Biographies

Mae Jemison

Space Pioneer

by Robert Kraske

Consultant:
James Gerard
Aerospace Education Specialist
Kennedy Space Center
Cape Canaveral, FL

Capstone
press

Mankato, Minnesota

Fact Finders is published by Capstone Press,
151 Good Counsel Drive, P.O. Box 669, Mankato, Minnesota 56002.
www.capstonepress.com

Library of Congress Cataloging-in-Publication Data
Kraske, Robert.
    Mae Jemison : space pioneer / by Robert Kraske.
    p. cm.—(Fact finders. Biographies)
    Includes bibliographical references and index.
    ISBN-13: 978-0-7368-6420-6 (hardcover)
    ISBN-10: 0-7368-6420-2 (hardcover)
    1. Jemison, Mae, 1956– —Juvenile literature. 2. African American women astronauts—
Biography—Juvenile literature. 3. Astronauts—United States—Biography—Juvenile
literature. I. Title. II. Series: Fact Finders. Biographies. Great African Americans.
TL789.85.J46K73 2007
629.450092—dc22   2005037569

Summary: An introduction to the life of Mae Jemison, the engineer and doctor who
    became the first African American woman to fly on the space shuttle.

Editorial Credits
John Bliss and Jennifer Murtoff (Navta Associates), editors; Juliette Peters, set designer;
    Lisa Zucker (Navta Associates), book designer; Wanda Winch, photo researcher/
    photo editor

Photo Credits
AP/Wide World Photos, 7; Corbis/Bettmann, 17; Corbis/Charles & Josette Lenars, 19;
Corbis/Matthew Mcvay, 14; Corbis/Sandy Felsenthal, 8; Courtesy of Morgan Park High
School, Chicago/Keith Majeske, 11; Courtesy of the Medical Center Archives of NewYork-
Presbyterian Hospital/Weill Cornell, 15 (both); Getty Images Inc./China Photos, 25; Getty
Images Inc./Robert Mora, 1, 26; Getty Images Inc./Tim Boyle, 13; NASA/Johnson Space
Center Collection, cover, 5 (both), 21, 22, 23, 27; Globe Photos, Inc./NBC, 9; SuperStock/
Karl Kummels, 18

Table of Contents

First into Space

Countdown! The last seconds ticked by. 5 . . . 4 . . . 3 . . . 2 . . . 1 . . .

Endeavour's big rockets blasted fire. The 78-ton (71-metric-ton) spaceship lifted off the launch pad. The thunder it made could be heard miles away. Up, up into the blue sky it rose.

Minutes later, *Endeavour* was flying 260 miles (418 kilometers) above Earth. Its speed was 17,500 miles (28,160 kilometers) per hour, faster than a rifle bullet.

Endeavour carried seven astronauts. One was Mae Jemison. As a girl, Jemison dreamed of flying in space. On September 12, 1992, she became the first African American woman astronaut.

Jemison flew into space on *Endeavour*'s first mission in 1992.

Jemison posed in her space suit before her historic flight.

Chapter 2

Early Years

Mae Carol Jemison was born on October 17, 1956, in Decatur, Alabama. Her father was a carpenter who built houses. Her mother cleaned homes.

When Jemison was three, she moved to Chicago with her mother, father, brother Ricky, and sister Ada Sue. They lived in an apartment on the South Side in an African American neighborhood.

FACT!

Jemison's mother got her college education in Chicago. She became a teacher. She taught in Chicago public schools for 25 years.

Jemison grew up in Chicago, shown here as it looked in 1960.

Even as a child, Jemison knew what she wanted to do. At McCosh Elementary School, her kindergarten teacher asked, "What do you want to be when you grow up?" Hands flew up. "Fireman." "Nurse." Jemison called out, "Scientist!"

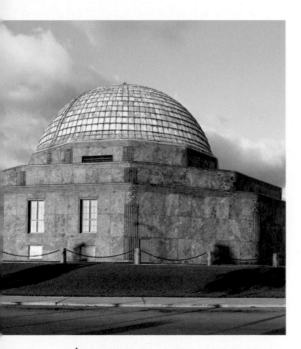

↑ Chicago's Adler Planetarium inspired Jemison to learn about the universe.

Blinking Stars

As a child, Jemison liked to go to the Adler **Planetarium**. It showed stars shining in the night sky. She was fascinated by the stars, the planets, and the universe.

Jemison had questions. How far away were the stars? Why did they blink? Could people live on other planets?

To find answers, Jemison began to read science books from the public library. She wondered why the scientists in the stories were often white men.

Then Jemison watched a TV program called *Star Trek*. The program showed men and women of different races. They traveled together in space and worked together. She read *A Wrinkle in Time*, a book by Madeline L'Engle. The main characters were women scientists. These stories helped her realize that women, too, could become scientists.

In *Star Trek*, ➡ men and women of all races worked together in space.

Another Move

One day, Jemison's parents told her that the family was moving. Teenage gangs were fighting in the streets. The neighborhood had become too rough.

The family moved to a safer neighborhood. Jemison went to Esmond Elementary School in Chicago. There she skipped seventh grade and went to eighth grade. Her test scores were higher than those of some students in high school.

Drawing and Math

In 1969, Jemison entered Morgan Park High School. She was 12 years old. In high school, she discovered interests other than science. Jemison told teachers she wanted to be an **engineer**. She became the first girl to take drafting classes at her school. She learned to draw parts for machines.

▲ Morgan Park High School is one of the highest-rated schools in Chicago.

Jemison also developed strong math skills. On school mornings before classes began, she met with her math teacher, Mr. Drymiller. He prepared her for the advanced math she would take in college.

Chapter 3

Young Scientist

In her junior year, Jemison began a science project. She studied a blood disease called **sickle-cell anemia**. After school, she went to Cook County Hospital. She talked with doctors about the disease. She read books in the Illinois Institute of Technology library. Her project won first place at a science fair.

In 1973, Jemison graduated from Morgan Park High School. She was 16 years old. She scored high on tests to enter college. Four schools offered her **scholarships**. She chose Stanford University in California.

Jemison learned about sickle-cell anemia from the doctors at Cook County Hospital.

Jemison moved from Chicago to Stanford University in California to go to college. ▼

Young College Student

Jemison was one of the youngest students at Stanford. She took classes in **chemical engineering** and in African American studies. She also learned to speak Swahili, an African language.

Jemison often sat in the front row in class. She liked to ask questions and to challenge her teachers. One teacher called her one of the most outstanding students he had met in 25 years of teaching.

FACT!

Jemison speaks English, Swahili, Russian, and Japanese.

Jemison studied to be a doctor at Cornell University. Jemison's class picture was taken at Cornell in 1981.

Jemison graduated from Stanford in 1977. She decided to become a doctor. She went to Cornell University in New York City.

Why did Jemison go to medical school after engineering school? She wanted to apply her engineering skills to understanding how our bodies work. She studied **biomedical engineering**. Often she would study until two o'clock in the morning.

Chapter 4

The New Doctor

After four years at Cornell, Jemison became a doctor. She worked at the Los Angeles County Hospital in California. She treated people with many different diseases.

In 1983, Jemison joined the Peace Corps. The Peace Corps sends volunteers to poor countries to train farmers, teachers, and medical workers. Jemison went to Sierra Leone and Liberia in West Africa.

QUOTE

"Each one of us has the right and the responsibility to live up to our individual potential and ambitions."

—Mae Jemison

▲ Jemison worked as a doctor in Los Angeles before she traveled to Africa with the Peace Corps.

Unclean Water

Jemison visited poor people living in mud huts. Goats and chickens walked inside the huts. Villages had open sewers. Jemison found that many people were drinking unclean water. Harmful germs in the water made people sick. Clean water, she learned, was as important as medicine to treat sick people.

Jemison taught people in Africa the importance of clean water. ▼

▲ Many of the people Jemison met in Sierra Leone lived in huts like this one.

Jemison finished work in West Africa in 1985. She returned to Los Angeles and worked as a doctor. At night, she took classes in engineering at the University of California. There was always more to learn.

QUOTE

"I learned that no matter what I did, I could not be scared."
—Mae Jemison

Chapter 5

Flying High

One day Jemison read a newspaper story. NASA, the U.S. space agency, was looking for astronauts. She mailed in her application in October 1985.

Then in January 1986, the *Challenger* space shuttle exploded. The accident happened only 73 seconds after it lifted off the launch pad. All seven astronauts on board were killed.

But Jemison was not afraid. The *Challenger* accident made her want to find a safer way to fly in space. In 1987, NASA chose 15 out of 2,000 people to train as astronauts. Jemison was one of them. She was an "intelligent, sincere, and stable young woman," said one NASA worker.

Jemison was one of seven crew members to fly on the space shuttle *Endeavour*.

Jemison's love of learning prepared her for the training she would need before she was ready to fly. Her work paid off, and she was assigned to a crew on the space shuttle *Endeavour*.

▲ Nan Davis and Mae Jemison conducted experiments on *Endeavour*.

Circling Earth

Endeavour lifted off safely. Jemison spent the next eight days in space. She and the other scientists on *Endeavour* carried out experiments.

Jemison tried to answer questions about the lack of gravity in space. She and the other scientists did experiments to find out if tadpoles would develop normally without gravity. Jemison hatched the tadpoles and watched them grow. Her experiments helped scientists understand how living things react to the lack of gravity.

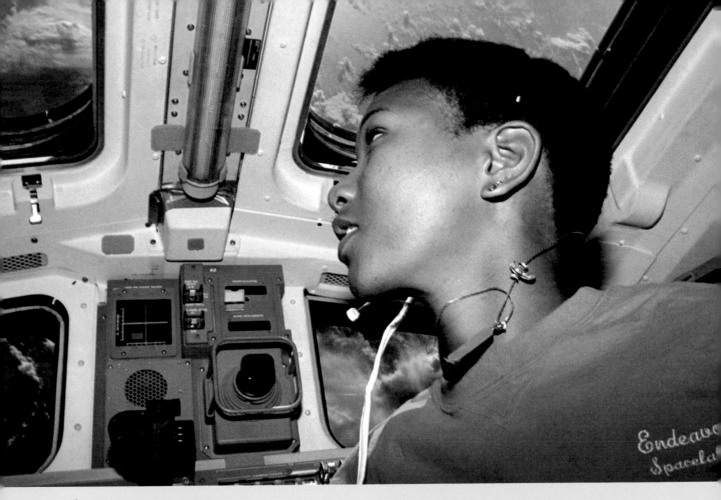

▲ High over the Earth,
Jemison looked down
on her home.

From the shuttle, Jemison saw that
Earth had a shimmering glow around
it. She thought about how strong but
vulnerable Earth looked. She realized
that people need to treat Earth with
respect. She said, "We're not going
to solve our problems by going to a
different planet."

23

Chapter 6

Asking Questions

In 1994, Jemison began a science camp in the United States called The Earth We Share (TEWS). Students from around the world come to the camp. They ask questions and talk about the problems we face on Earth. How many people can Earth support? How can we make sure that everyone has enough food and water?

"Science," Jemison tells TEWS students, "is about not knowing. It's all right to say I don't know, but let's try to find out."

The students try to come up with solutions. Then they return to their own countries. They talk with other people about what they have learned.

Jemison uses her experience as an astronaut to encourage students to ask questions about the problems on Earth.

In 1994, Jemison also started The Jemison Group in Houston, Texas. Her company helps improve the lives of people in West Africa. She is the president of the organization.

"My life, I imagine and hope, continues to hold secrets, new challenges, and good times."
—Mae Jemison

Jemison is always looking forward to the future and the opportunities ahead. ➤

Final Questions

When Jemison talks to students, she asks them what they want to do with their lives. She asks them how they plan to do it.

Dr. Mae Jemison knew what she wanted to do. She became an engineer, a doctor, an astronaut, and a company president. Who knows what she may do next? "What we do with our talents is up to each one of us," she says.

Fast Facts

Full name: Mae Carol Jemison

Birth: October 17, 1956

Birthplace: Decatur, Alabama

Parents: Dorothy and Charlie Jemison

Siblings: Ricky and Ada Sue

Hometown: Chicago, Illinois, now Houston, Texas

Education: Bachelor of Science in chemical engineering, Stanford University, 1977; Doctorate in medicine, Cornell University, 1981

Achievements:

First African American woman in space, 1992

National Women's Hall of Fame, 1993

Founder, The Jemison Group, 1994

Founder, The Earth We Share, 1994

Time Line

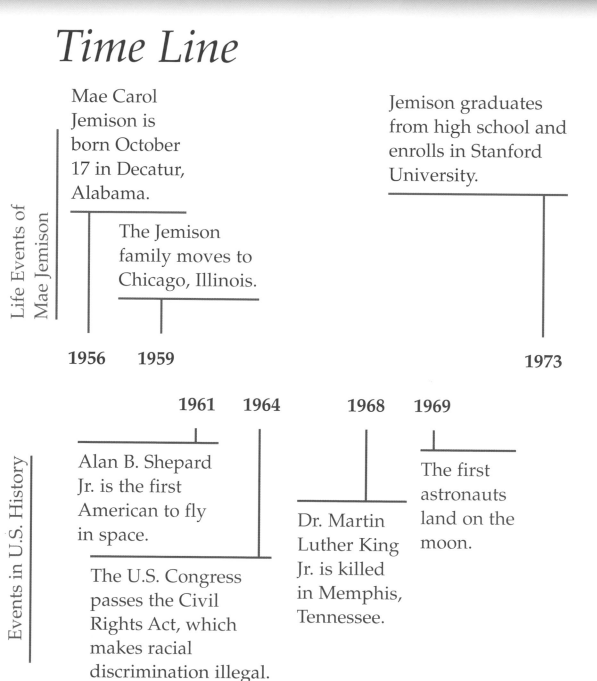

Life Events of Mae Jemison

Mae Carol Jemison is born October 17 in Decatur, Alabama.

The Jemison family moves to Chicago, Illinois.

Jemison graduates from high school and enrolls in Stanford University.

1956   **1959**   **1973**

1961   **1964**   **1968**   **1969**

Events in U.S. History

Alan B. Shepard Jr. is the first American to fly in space.

The U.S. Congress passes the Civil Rights Act, which makes racial discrimination illegal.

Dr. Martin Luther King Jr. is killed in Memphis, Tennessee.

The first astronauts land on the moon.

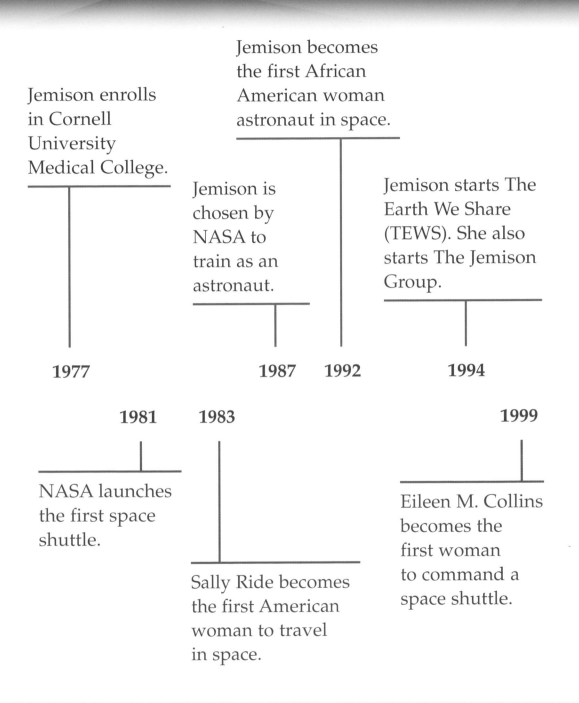

Jemison enrolls in Cornell University Medical College.

Jemison becomes the first African American woman astronaut in space.

Jemison is chosen by NASA to train as an astronaut.

Jemison starts The Earth We Share (TEWS). She also starts The Jemison Group.

1977

1987 **1992**

1994

1981 **1983**

1999

NASA launches the first space shuttle.

Sally Ride becomes the first American woman to travel in space.

Eileen M. Collins becomes the first woman to command a space shuttle.

Glossary

biomedical engineering (bi-oh-MED-uh-kuhl en-juh-NIHR-ing)—the activity of applying engineering science to biological research and health care

chemical engineering (KEM-uh-kuhl en-juh-NIHR-ing)—the activity of applying chemistry to solve practical problems

engineer (en-juh-NIHR)—someone who is trained to design and build machines, vehicles, bridges, roads, or other structures

planetarium (plan-uh-TAIR-ee-uhm)—a building with equipment for projecting the positions and movements of the sun, moon, planets, and stars onto a curved ceiling

scholarship (SKOL-ur-ship)—a grant or prize that pays for a student to go to college or to follow a course of study

sickle-cell anemia (SIK-uhl sel uh-NEE-mee-uh)—a condition in which red blood cells take on a sickle shape and cannot carry oxygen

vulnerable (VUHL-nur-uh-buhl)—in a weak position and likely to be hurt or damaged in some way

Internet Sites

FactHound offers a safe, fun way to find Internet sites related to this book. All of the sites on FactHound have been researched by our staff.

Here's how:

1. Visit *www.facthound.com*

2. Choose your grade level.

3. Type in this book ID **0736864202** for age-appropriate sites. You may also browse subjects by clicking on letters, or by clicking on pictures and words.

4. Click on the **Fetch It** button.

FactHound will fetch the best sites for you!

Read More

Gelletly, LeeAnne. *Mae Jemison.* Black Americans of Achievement. Philadelphia: Chelsea House, 2002.

Jemison, Mae. *Find Where the Wind Goes: Moments from My Life.* New York: Scholastic, 2001.

Naden, Corinne J., **and Rose Blue.** *Mae Jemison: Out of This World.* A Gateway Biography. Brookfield, Conn.: Millbrook Press, 2003.

Index

DATE DUE

DEMCO 38-297